Success with Scola:
Building Direct Sales One Solid Brick at a Time

By: Lisa Scola

Success with Scola:
Building Direct Sales One Solid Brick at a Time

Success with Scola:
Building Direct Sales One Solid Brick at a Time

ISBN-13: 978-1727420340
ISBN-10: 1727420349

Dedication

This book is dedicated to the memory of my mom, Carolee. She was my best friend, supporter, and cheerleader. Also, to my children, Zackary, Mikayla, and John. I have made it where I am in business and in life because of my drive to be the best I can be. This I do for my children.

I also want to dedicate my compassion to you, the reader. If you love what you do as much as I love what I do, then you are on your way to Success! Hard work, determination, and consistency-and you will be on your way to living your dreams.

Table of Contents

~Prospecting~
"You don't have to be great to start, but you have to start to be great"
-73-

~Leadership~
"Be the leader YOU would follow"
-79-

~Making it a Family Business~
"Make it a family business."
-87-

~Fundraising~
"Small actions times a lot of people equals big change"
-95-

~Success~
"Success is not the key to happiness, Happiness is the key to Success"
-101-

Your Resources for Adjusting Your Sales
-105-

Introduction

Striving for Success is a life effort. Whether you are starting up a home-based business, just starting a career, wanting more for your family a student or you're an athlete. We all want to be a Success. In this book, I share my personal struggles along my path to Success, not only in life and being a mom but in my home-based business as well. We all have obstacles and I have had my share of good and bad that have affected my life.

I have taken a hobby and turned it into a multimillion-dollar business, turning dreams into realities and proving to myself that finding my own financial independence is rewarding and worth the time and effort needed to accomplish it. I was told you can make excuses, or you can make money, and that phrase holds very true in building a business. It's also true that self-employed people will quit a 40 hour a week job to work 80 hours for themselves, because being your own boss is far more rewarding than working for someone else and making them money. I hope you enjoy reading what I shared and can take something to help you apply to your own life and get you on that path of Success, the path that only you can create while following you're dreams.

~Life the Beginning~
Live every day like it's your last

Life from the day your born, that day when everything you will become in your lifetime begins. I know my life started out great, as many, I had a mom and dad. Now not everyone starts out with a mom and dad. You may have started with just a mom. Or maybe neither, maybe you were given to adoptive parents to be your family. No matter how that day started one thing is for sure, you were given life and a journey was about to begin.

I have learned a lot on my journey so far, one thing is that it really doesn't matter how much money you are raised with or how many brothers or sisters you have or how great your education is. Wanting success in life has everything to do with you, and how much you want something.

We can all go through our lives blaming others for the short comings we see in ourselves. But honestly let's take a good look at that. Maybe your youth wasn't all you thought it should be, and well geez it certainly wasn't as good as say your neighbors or your friends at school. Or your family didn't have much money, or maybe you had too much money. Your mom just wasn't home much, and your dad wasn't emotionally supportive. There are so many factors that we all want to look at and use as excuses for why we are not the person we really wanted to be when we grew up.

When I was growing up I had what I thought was a very normal life. I was an only child and was raised with many traditions, I had a ½ sister and ½ brother, but they didn't live with us, my parents gave me just about everything I wanted. My father always made great money and mom stayed home with me. Coming from an Italian background most everything was based around food and alcohol. My father always got very involved in anything I wanted to do, if I showed an interest in something it immediately became a project. Not always a bad thing but I did learn that if I wasn't really interested in it don't say anything about it because my dad will have me enrolled with instructors on a path that I really didn't care to take.

At 6 years old, not only did my father take me ice skating, but he made sure I learned to skate, he purchased a pair of skates for me and signed me up with a personal instructor and I was on my way to a nice ice-skating career. That was my first journey in my life, I spent the better part of my adolescents on the Ice and dreamt about going to the Olympics. My parents enrolled me in dance and gymnastics to help with the skating and I traveled to compete in competitions all over. My skating career came to an end at 15 years old when my parents went through a terrible divorce. My mom and I were left to make life work and so many things in my life changed overnight. I stopped Ice Skating and I started working at McDonalds at 15 ½ I changed my high school course to office and business instead of college, so I could get work that was full time. I truly didn't resent this life style change because I was able to help my mom and our household, but it was a big change in direction from where I thought I was heading.

After graduating from High School, I went off to a trade school in Pittsburgh, PA called Wilma Boyd School of Business and Travel. It was cool to live in such a beautiful city for a few months and have a taste of living on my own with roommates. I did amazing at this school and really wanted to work in the travel industry and move to Florida to start my life. Well at the end of school, the job that was offered to me was in Chicago. I was going to have to live with at least three or four people just to survive and it seemed scary and I suppose I just wasn't ready to make that kind of move. I was also dating my boyfriend from High School again so of course going back home seemed liked the right thing to do. Thinking back its funny that I can't remember my mom being disappointed at all. I do although remember her trying to convince me to go and try it, but like I say now I was young and dumb and thought I knew everything. So, home I came.

I then decided I may want to go to college for nursing or psychology. Well I did a few semesters at college but that just wasn't for me, so I decided to just continue working, I loved working and I loved having money. I have had several different types of jobs, mostly all clerical and assistant work, I have always been a quick learner and I was never afraid to try anything. I was even given the opportunity to be an ice-skating Instructor for a few years which by the way I absolutely loved doing, but a few years into that all the sports politics got in the way of my wanting to continue.

I ended up married at 25 and I started a family of my own. I had my son Zackary at 28 years old and when it was time to go back to work they had gotten rid of my job here and moved it to Akron, Ohio which was a nice commute that I wasn't willing to drive. So, opted to take the lay off and stay home with my son. I had my daughter Mikayla 2 ½ years after Zack and loved being just a stay at home mom. Although I was feeling that I should be doing so much more with my life and really felt like I needed more. This is what started my direct sales career. My two children at the time where 3 ½ and 1 and I knew working from home would both satisfy the need to get out of the house and play adult and give the family some extra money along the way. My stay at home business really started off slow. Well I say slow because the first 2 years I was really my own personal shopper. I did all the training available and I could see the possibilities, but I was slow to get it really going. I just wasn't "hungry" enough as they say. But after 2 years I decided to give it more attention and make it more a business rather than a hobby.

The decision was brought on because a friend of mine at the time asked me about it. She wanted to make some money and thought this opportunity would work well for her. Honestly, it's a familiar story to many.

Here I am just dabbing around in this business and a good friend of mine asked me if I was making any money with the business. I really wasn't making any money yet, but I see the potential and I had met a bunch of people that were really doing great with it. I also knew that I wanted to make more money with it and to have a friend join me to start the next step in my business seemed so perfect! So, as you would expect I told her "yes of course I'm making money" and I quickly needed to find out how to get someone signed up! After contacting the local manager, I was pointed in the right direction and I got my first personal team member! I was excited about it and I knew there was so much more I needed to look into now if I wanted to go in this direction with my little stay-at-home business. Off I went…and boom! Suddenly, I had a growing home-based business that was making me some money.

You may be thinking to yourself "oh sure as if it is that simple" well it really is that simple. I just never stopped asking people. I placed classified ads and I put our company's brochures everywhere I went. I used recruiting fliers and anything else I could find to get my name out. Social media was not a thing then and I had to rely on the "old fashion way" of recruiting. Which may I add still works amazingly today. Direct Sales is all about relationships, clearly if people like you it makes it easier to offer them a service. And I felt I was offering a great service!

Regardless of the Direct Sales company they all have the same basic plan. Meet people, offer them what you have to offer and either make them a customer or sign them up and have them join your team! Easy peasy right!?

Now the funny thing about life is that it is ever changing. We experience so many different life events throughout our lives, we are constantly having to "go with the flow" or "bend and twist." I've heard it said many times "adjust our sails" for all that comes to us. There is sickness, death, tragedies with weather, unforeseen accidents etc. Also, we have great things that happen like births, family additions, moves, personal achievements and so on.

I however experienced divorce, a life changing and very dilapidating event. At the time, I had 3 children, yes, I had added another one. My oldest son Zack was 7, my daughter Mikayla 5 and my youngest son John 1 years old. I will not go into all the details of this because these events don't need any kind of explanation but know that this was as many divorces are a gloomy time in my life. My thriving direct selling business started to go down, everything around me felt like it was just caving in around me. As any tragic event, you feel like there is no end, no beginning or anything in between.

Life does not prepare us for events that are tragic, life doesn't prepare us for the good either when you think about. We all must live and learn, and the difference in the outcome is how we handle it. How we see the next day or even the next minute. A lot of times we may need to break down the days into minutes just to survive. However, we do it, finding the solution is the key. Getting to that next phase of life should be the plan.

For me I have always learned from my mom who was the best example of strength, that you just don't quit. "Money is something you can't take with you when you die" and "there is no debtor's prison." These where all phrases my mom used often while I was growing up. Now she was very on point with just about everything and I was so lucky to have her. What life tries to teach you and I learned along the way was the same words from my mom and that's to never GIVE UP – which really does mean NEVER QUIT!

At this point in my life I had to take a good look at where I was. My mom had health issues that were getting worse, my Dad who left when I was 15 was still nowhere around and I had 3 beautiful children to take care of.

So now to decide what I am I going to do with my life. Ha and to think here I am at 36 years of age and life is so ever changing. I thought I had it all figured out. Married with my children, a good life (or at least I thought it was) and a direct sales business that was going to make all the difference in our coming years. See there are no promises on that day we are born. The only promise we have is that single moment. At an anytime our lives can change, it can change when we are born. It can change when we are young or when we are young adults. Our health can change, an accident can change our life. A person can come into our lives and make it change. No promises! Why is it so many of us live our lives like someone owes us? Why do we think we are better than that person sitting right next to you? What makes us think that we have it all figured out? My life changed overnight and believe me I wasn't very happy about having to refigure my already figured out life.

Well I like many of you right now, I had a good support system in my life. As I do today. I feel having a good support system is what makes all the difference many times. No not family support, although my mom was there for me as she has always been my entire life, but she was not well, and I knew I wouldn't have her around the earth with me much longer. I had a few good friends and they are the ones that don't let you quit. The ones that drag you out of bed and point you in the right direction. If you don't have a few of those in your life I highly suggest you find a couple.

Take a few minutes and write down your support system:

So here I am refiguring life, not making enough money to pay my bills and support my kids. I needed to pay for a divorce and clear up all the debt that my ex left for me to pay and my children to take care of. I was literally drowning, and I needed to get income and the days where just going by. Now do I want to go get a J.O.B (to me stands for *just over broke*) or maybe take advantage of going back to school. Well as I said earlier I didn't care for the school thing then, probably won't like it now. Then another life changing event happened.

My oldest son Zackary really wanted me home still. I mentioned to him that I was going to consider getting a *J.O.B.* and he really didn't like that at all. He said, "who is going to be here when I go to school in the morning" and "who is going to be here when I get home." It was a complete eye opener, see they were going through enough change at the time and It broke my heart to think of leaving them especially now.

I have this business and I know it can make money, good money! Life changing money! So now to make that decision, and in life really when you want something all you need to do is to decide to do it! Make that decision and then DO IT.

So, I needed to put on those big girl panties. I went back to the basic building skills I had learned in the first few years of my direct selling career. I began to build my business back up again. This however is not the easiest thing to do, it takes time and commitment. It takes falling and getting back up. Making calls, putting in the hours, talking to as many people as I could. One day at a time my life was getting back to my life again.

You first need to always realize that a business isn't built in 1 week, or 1 month or even 1 year. Businesses take time to build. One thing I see all the time repeatedly is that someone wants to start a home-based business and they expect that in less than 1 year or even in 2 or 3 years they should be at the top! Oh, and they also don't think they should have to invest much money let alone time in it.

Well, if this is you, then yes, I'm talking to you - it doesn't happen quickly. Now when moving forward without taking anything away that you're doing and adding more things to it you will find progress, a lot of progress. But it truly takes time and if someone is offering you an opportunity and is telling you that in little to no time you will be making all kinds of money, they are probably lying. I suggest you talk to a few other people.

Everyone has a story in their life, one that is just theirs and many may be very similar, but they are still different in many ways. I love to share mine with others because I have lived a lot of life so far, personally and professionally. I know there will be more and more to discover but thus far this is my story. This is how I have learned to combine Life, my business and Leadership into making the best out of all situations moving forward.

What I love most about life is that the learning adventures that I get every day are blessings to be on this thing called earth. I meet new people every day and enjoy having the open mind that it takes to accept them no matter what they want out of their lives. The most beautiful thing about the world is the change. It is what will make these next few chapters hopefully insightful enough for you to take something from it and make a change in your own life and business. I know, I have read many books that have given me so much to think about. Tools to use in my business and in my life. Learning is something that we never stop doing. And if you do stop learning then that means you have stopped living which gives very little meaning to everyday as we know it.

Think of your WHY! Write it down, SHARE it, and make it REAL!

~Breaking it All Down~

"Dreams can inspire you, but goals can change your life"

Breaking it down; your goals are going to be the number one key to your success. Most of the time our vision is so broad that we need to a lot of times break down our goals to smaller stepping stones in reaching our goals.

I have done this and continue to do this, knowing that one of my goals is financial independence that is something that isn't going to happen overnight. And financial independence is different for everyone. In my case I want to know that I can pay all my bills, have a savings and travel without ever wondering if I will have the money. I never want to be broke again.

I have lived my life most of it anyways paycheck to paycheck. Even at the age of 15 when my parents divorced It was the way my mom and I survived. It was pretty much normal for me and I have seen in my years now of living that it is basically normal for the average home.

Well I don't want to be "a normal home" and I'm positive you don't either since you are reading this book, that you don't want that normal home either. Well there are some steps I want to share with you that have worked well for me to break the normal home stigma. I will share first the merry go round of money.

I know for myself that this starts with not making enough money to pay all the bills that you have in your life. We are not born with these bills, we have acquired them through living and I have learned that society teaches us to live outside of our financial means. I had to take a long hard look at this when I went through my divorce. I was left with all the credit card debt to take care of on my own and a house that I had to sell out of foreclosure along with my 3 kids to raise. Many adults when faced with divorce or separation will take on the responsibility of paying for their past debts and children together, because this is not uncommon unfortunately and as adults they still learn to take responsibility through the change, but my ex did not. He made it clear that he wanted me to lose everything including my kids. This not only gave me the fuel I needed to change my life around to be the success I knew I could be, but it helped me show my children that no matter what happens in life you can make a difference if you have the will to do so.

I know that many others go through divorces or even become widowed or have a life changing events happen that is beyond our control. That is another reason why I want to share how important it is no matter how your life is today, to make sure that you are stable. That you can sustain yourself and your household and family whether you're with a partner or not.

This type of situation I was in can shut a person down completely and they will give up. Well I decided a long time ago that I wasn't going to be a victim of circumstance. And that I will come out on top one way or another! It's a decision that you must make in life, no matter the hardship it is your ultimate decision to make it better. I started by breaking down the debt, and little by little I started to pay it all off. It takes time and a plan to do this. You also cannot add to the debt during this time. As hard as it is, you need to say no! You need to buckle down and live as small as you can. This is a temporary situation for long term success.

Always look at the big picture and not where you are at that moment. Keep the dream board up so you can see what you are working for. And share the successes of getting out of debt with your support system! As you start to see the end of it all the freedom you feel is like no other. Now you will also see your business start booming as well. A lot of times the financial debt and despair will hold us back from the point we need to be at.

Write down some debt you want gone:

Now write down how much more money you need a month to pay it off:

At this point you can now start investing even more in your business and you will start noticing a change in your life and all your goals. I know when I finally started rebuilding my credit, it took about 6 years before I was able to get my first charge account. This was one of those yearly fee charges and as much as I didn't like the fee I was willing to show that creditor and prove to myself that I could build this bad credit back up to good again.

In direct sales, you need to be able to set that goal. All the sales charts are different depending on your direct selling company, so I can't really put together a plan for you, but I know that with my direct sales business I put a 2-week plan together.

Break your sales down by customers, and order sizes or even parties if that is what you do. You are the only one that knows how much money you need to make, and you will be the only person that can set this sales goal to be sure you are making the money you need to pay your bills and invest more in your business. Now take a break and write down your plan, write down your customers, average orders and the percentage of earnings you will have.

Use your commission charts to start a plan:

Now that you have finally done some planning let's move forward to how you are making that plan and how that plan will change the longer you are in business for yourself. Also look at your company's compensation plan and bonuses. Are you taking advantage of everything your direct sales company is offering?

Another story because I love to share personal stories as we move forward and this one truly touched my heart so deeply and was just one more affirmation that I was moving in the right direction with my direct sales business. As I have shared so far, I was going through a very ugly divorce, I had no money. I mean no money! My mom had already stretched her monetary help to me as much as she possibly could, and Christmas was right around the corner.

My oldest son Zack as I have said, at the time was 7 and all my kids were very excited for Santa to make a visit just as he always had their entire life so far. Now I could have told them that it was going to be a year without a Santa Claus, but I just couldn't do that. I needed to figure out how to make that Christmas morning special for them just like it always has been. Having no idea how this was going to happen I just continued to bust my butt and work double hard with my sales and my team.

Well there was an incentive going on like there usually is in direct sales, especially with the company I'm involved in. I was aware of the incentives but also so consumed with just building my business that I really wasn't following any progress towards this one.

I'm a big believer in just working the business, and if you work the business you will achieve goals that are in place by doing what you are supposed to be doing anyways. So, Christmas is a few weeks away and I've been able to get a few items for the kids so I'm not feeling totally defeated at this point. Although I know they will be expecting more because that is how they had been raised thus far. Well just then I received a phone call from my manager at the time, she was excited and totally over the moon to give me this awesome news. My manager Anita was more than a manager to me, she was like part of my family and still is to this day. I had no idea why she was so excited but ok I will take it; good news didn't come easy to me these days. She asked me if I was aware of the incentive going on and I asked her which one lol, and she clarified it was a leadership incentive. Now with the company I'm with they had started to make some new changes at the time to help growth and one of the changes they made where bonuses for title advancement among others. When they made the changes, it made it a bit easier to move up and I was working towards that, so I could make more money.

I will never forget the feeling in my stomach when she told me I had just earned $1,500 and that I should be receiving it with our next pay which would happen before Christmas!!! I just cried. It was like a miracle but not really a miracle because I was working hard for my business! And this was a well-earned award, I worked hard for it.

I went shopping on Christmas eve, I bought some gifts my kids really wanted for Christmas and I got them wrapped and under the tree that night! Now I didn't spend all the money on gifts, remember I'm working to raise these kids on my own for the most part so a good portion paid bills, too.

Christmas morning when my son Zack woke up early like he has always done, and he went out to see if Santa came he was very surprised. Later that day he actually said to me and I quote "mommy I know there is a Santa for sure! I know because there is NO WAY you could afford to buy us anything this year" my heart was full.
You see the beauty of Christmas isn't the gifts, truly it's the magic. I'm not a material kind of person but my kids were going through so much already with our divorce. The changes they had to go through were enough already and this just made it better, it made it easier to swallow. My kids could have a belief one more year and because of my business I was able to make it happen.

You see when I tell people that there is money to be made in Direct Sales and that you need to take advantage of ALL THE EARNINGS they offer, this is one of the reasons why. Bonuses are an avenue to reinvest, to make things happen that you may not have been able to afford without them.

This is what I want you to learn moving forward!

What are incentives within your company that could help you?

What are you doing to earn these incentives?

~Goal Setting~
"If you fail to plan, your planning to fail"

Goal setting is first and foremost the most important part of any successes. I have talked a little about my growing up, my failed marriage and my direct sales business that I about lost through it all. I fortunately had many years of self-help support that really did help me through a lot of what I went through especially my divorce. I again always suggest you find a good support system, one that holds you accountable for your growth.

I believe the one area I know I wasn't failing on was being a mom, and the most important thing to me was making a household that was happy and stress free. It's not that easy especially when you have such a dysfunctional divorce. I however never gave up and I'm so glad I didn't. Now my kids still have a lot of life left to live, but I know that one thing is certain, my never quitting attitude and my success in direct sales has left a good impression for my children. Now they have their own lives to mold and their own dreams to reach. I will sit back and enjoy watching them grow from all their own decisions.

Now what is your goal? What do you want out of your business? Your relationships? Write them down, look at them. How about breaking it down even further. What is your financial goal? Make two lists, one for your business and a personal one as well. Once you have made these two lists look at your business and put together a plan that will get you to reaching these goals both personal and for your business.

Take some time, think about these and write them down:

When I first started my direct sales business, I did it as a hobby not a business. I did the training offered but really wasn't into doing what it was going to take to make this business a success. One day a friend of mine inquired about my business. She was interested in starting to and wanted to know how to go about doing it. She also wanted to know if I was having any success in it because she really wanted to make some extra money.

This opened a new opportunity for me in direct sales, it made me look at their leadership opportunity. I jumped on the chance to get her started and to add her to my own team. Most people don't take advantage of this part of their direct sales business and I know many are set up a bit differently. I really don't care how its set up, if you're not doing this you really need to start today.

Recruiting people to join your business is something that can add residual income to your life. An income that will continue to pay you if you stay with your company, even long after you stop really working the business. Its Multi-Level Marketing or MLM. This is a great way to build a future income or legacy. I have learned in the time that I have been in Leadership that offering an extra income or a change in career paths for others is very rewarding, both personally and financially.

Building a team is not easy and takes persistence and the ability to continue to always add and train individuals to get exactly what they want from their own businesses. I have done this long enough to see many people come and go. I have seen people start recruiting but stop at one or two people. I have seen them make excuses why they aren't successful.

I have seen people start leadership, build a great foundation in both sales and leadership and then still up and quit. Giving it all up and going to work a job thinking that they will have more security to find out all these years later that they have went from job to job still searching. All the while my business has continued to grow and get bigger all because I have never given up on it.

Let me explain why I wouldn't and still don't give up. I have always, and I continue to look at the big picture. Just like life nothing is easy, we must work for what we want out of it. Unless your perfectly happy with a 9-5 job that has a boss that you go to work for everyday to make them more money, than an opportunity like direct sales or starting your own home-based business probably isn't for you.

You need to ask yourself what it is that you want out of life? Where do you want to be in a few years? Are you willing to do whatever it takes to reach your personal and professional goals? I mentioned earlier in this book that I thought I wanted to go to school. And believe me at the time of wondering what direct sales company I wanted to join. I also thought about going back to school and finishing college. My problem with this was the money I would be investing in college, and I wasn't guaranteed a good paying job when I finish. So, I'm going to put myself in more debt, take more time away from my kids and have no guarantee of work?

This didn't sound like something I really wanted and after really giving it some thought I came up with my own investment. Direct sales! My own home-based business that I can take money and reinvest in myself and in my business to get to where I want to be in the future. All while working at home around my kids schedules and my home life.

The best part was once I got involved in leadership and began building my team I was now earning bonuses and trips for all my hard work. Now don't get me wrong, you need to sacrifice just as if you were a freshman in college living on your own. You need to cut corners and to say the least you may be eating a lot of mac n cheese and ramen to make these goals achievable. But like I've said, "short term sacrifice for long term financial success."

Now this is residual income and all the money I decided to invest into myself and my business are now paying off. I'm not saying that furthering your education is a bad thing at all. I have many highly-educated people on my team. It just wasn't the path I felt would be worth it for me. I like many others I know, I have built my own empire and if I would have taken my 1st choice I would be working a job and I would have a salary cap on how much I will make. I love that I don't have a salary cap with owning my own business.

So, in goal setting let's make sure that you are taking advantage of everything your company has to offer. This will insure that you can put together a plan to reach the full potential you are offered. Every penny counts, and I believe if there is money being offered or a trip or anything else, make it a priority to earn everything you can. In working towards these incentives even if you don't earn them all you will always show growth while trying. Again, this is all part of building a good business, key word "growing."

In keeping with my story sharing here is another great story I want to share. This is also about an incentive and again I earned something without even being aware that I was tracking it. Sales is a huge part of every direct selling business. The companies depend on sales to have continued growth and we as Independent Representatives can also build on our sales to make the money needed to continue to grow our businesses. As I was building my team I was canvasing areas all the time. I was putting out brochures, buying extra products for vendor events and setting up anywhere that would let me.

I invested money in brochures, hundreds of them every two weeks so I could find new areas to put them in and more people to hand them out to. It seemed I would find customers daily. But the recruiting was much harder. Building a strong customer base was important. Besides I was getting very good at converting customers to team members once I had them sold on our products. Besides who doesn't love a good discount on their products, especially when they are using them all the time.

During this time my company once again was having a trip incentive bases on sales increase, I as usual currently was not really paying much attention because I was more worried about making money. So much to my surprise again I received a call from my manager. She again was very excited to inform me that I had earned a trip for 2 on a cruise to the Bahamas. Well I wasn't very excited about it because for one reason I had been on a cruise before and I didn't like it. And the second reason was that it meant I would be away from my kids and my baby wasn't even 1 yet so that didn't sound like a trip I wanted to take.

She was more than persuasive for me to go and she made a very good point while convincing me, that I had earned this and a cruise with our company is much different than a normal "vacation cruise." With much hesitation I decided to take it. I went on this all-expense paid trip with my company and the other achievers. WOW is all I can say, this was an experience I will never forget and from that point on I really wanted to earn every trip they had to offer.

The red carpet was rolled out! We were given gifts and more attention than I have ever received on vacation. Truly the most amazing thing I had thus far ever experienced, and I was so thankful that I didn't pass it up.

Working hard every day on building your business really has a lot of perks. Not only was I making more money, but I was earning extra incentives and trips! I have never heard of many jobs doing this for their employees. It made me even more sure that I was moving in the right direction.

Are there any incentives you want to earn? Write them here, plan.

~Accountability~

"Accountability is the glue that ties the commitment to the result"

Accountability is part of my business and I want to share how to make it a big part of yours. This will be the part of the book that you will take what you do and use your own business adjective. Figure out the part of your direct sales business that is consumable. The products that you offer that a customer will be needing to order more of in the future. You are going to want to really focus on these products.

Time to work on how your follow up is going to help you in building a nice sales business. Write down and always keep track of all your customers. You want names, address, phone numbers and email address. Get your customers to link up with you on all social media sights that you are on. These are all ways of keeping in touch with your clients.

Find out what you can offer to them that they will be able to use on a regular basis and need to replace frequently and write them down. You will also have those customers that buy other products or just buy occasionally. These customers are good customers as well.

Now just like before, break it down and work on how much money you need to make-and how you can do this with sales. You can start to pay all your bills and be able to invest back into your business just from your growing customer base.

Don't be shy!! This will not make you any money. Are you afraid to offer your products to everyone? Well this needs to stop today. You need to talk to everyone everywhere you go. Offer your services with your business and fit your products into their lives. If they can't afford it, then they may make a great business partner which is a win for both of you. You will gain a team member and she will get her products at a discount and earn some extra money herself.

I had a friend of mine when I first started in leadership that was a consistent customer. She always ordered the core products and she loved them. One day I asked her if she was interested in a small discount on them and she replied, "tell me more." I explained that having her own account she would be able to save money on everything she loved so much and if anyone ordered from her she would literally get her products for free. She signed up, not only did she love the discount but with the extra money from orders at her job she was able to help pay for all kinds of things that came up in her own household. See I didn't lose a customer I gained an excellent team member.

Look now your business is growing! When I started to treat my business like a business and not a hobby, I found that scheduling became very important. How could I expect family members and other people to take me seriously if I was spending most of my time not working on my business. I have seen and heard all the life situations that will hold us back on success.

When you decide to work from home and you are truly at home and not working another job, you will need to have a schedule of what you want to accomplish every day and stick to that. Otherwise you can get caught up in cleaning, or soap operas or just plain spending too much time on your computer with social media. How about all the Netflix shows or what everyone else feels you should be doing for them since your home. We can fall into these bad habits but let me tell you now none of this is going to build your business. This is your business and you need to let everyone know that you have responsibilities with it every day. You need to make calls, you need to get out of the house and off Facebook to find customers. If your direct sales company is one that is more hostess based, then you need to be setting up those parties. Following up with your hostesses and making sure that they are inviting as many people as they can. Don't ever leave your business success up to someone else. I can tell you that no one will be as concerned with it as you are.

Now get out that planner and start planning. Let's start with the family; put appointments in the planner for doctors and school etc. Make a starting time every day. My business pretty much repeats itself every two weeks on things I need to do every two weeks during our selling schedule. I take care of sales and team training. I like to set time aside for prospecting which is both customers and recruits. Remember these go hand in hand, both will grow your business and when out talking to people you should be finding out what their needs are and offer either.

One thing I learned very early on in having a home-based business is making it part of my lifestyle. Adding what I do in my everyday life makes it easier to remember to do it. Always have your material with you. Always be ready to offer a brochure. And the biggest secret to being successful is getting their follow up information. After all this is your business and you want them as a customer or team member. So be sure you have some way to contact them once you walk away.

This will give you a 99% greater chance of getting an order from them in the future. Remember people are busy and even if what you are offering is exactly what they need, they will go home and forget. It's your job to follow up with them.

The first time I did my follow up calls I was so surprised by the results! I really didn't like to call people up, I felt that I was bugging them, and I also felt that if they were really interested they would call me. My manager was a great mentor for me. Since when I started my business I didn't start with another representative I was directed to the area "manager" and at the time that happened a lot. Now every direct sales business including the one I'm with is all leader based.

My manager Anita would always ask me "Lisa have you called your customers"? I would always respond the same way "no I'm pretty sure if they wanted something they would call me." Well finally I took her advice, I sat down one afternoon and decided to call everyone I had given a brochure to. I was so nervous I can remember praying to get everyone's answering machine lol. I dialed that first number and heard "hello" OH NO my hands were sweaty, and I almost forgot who I called. Immediately I said hello and asked for my customer. A few seconds later she was on the phone and I opened my conversation with a hey, how are you? And asked if she had a chance to look at the brochure. I was so surprised at all the wonderful responses I got, many of the calls I made did have orders for me and they were so happy I called. A few didn't need anything, but I offered up some samples for items they could try and a new brochure for next time and that worked out well too. I could not believe that I added an additional $240 to my order! This was big at the time because I really didn't have a very big customer base so to add this much in sales just by making follow up calls really surprised me.

That really got me excited to continue the follow up. I learned a few things from this experience; first I learned that I wasn't bothering people when I called them, they were excited to hear from me. I also learned how to set some goals with sales by giving myself an amount to work towards and raising that bar every time I placed an order.

For instance, as an example: if I had 20 customers I gave brochures to that I had follow up information on, I set a goal to get at least a $25 order from them. Many ordered more than that and some ordered less. Make an average so it works out. To do this take the total amount of your order and divide it by how many customers ordered. This will give you an average. Now in holding yourself accountable, figure out how much you need to earn to pay a bill or all the bills. Once you have worked out how much you are making now you can start planning out a sales budget.

An example: I wanted to earn $400.00 profit every two weeks. Our commission earns us 40% at a $500.00 or more order. Since some of the items I sell are also fixed earnings *which means we only get 20%* I liked to base my goal on 30%.

I needed a $1500.00 order. 1,500 divided by 50 customers is an average order $30.00. At 30% earnings that a $450.00 profit!

Set a goal for yourself. Hold yourself accountable to reach it and do what you need to do make it happen. If you're not making enough money with your business and this is what you want to do, then what is it you need? More customers or larger customer orders. Either way you can do it!

Make a list now of 50 customers:

I never believed it was possible to earn money in direct sales. Before getting involved in this kind of business I was like everyone else, working for that paycheck. The paycheck was always the same unless I was given a raise or able to work some over time. Every two weeks I had the same amount of money to work with. This works great if you don't change your budget or add any extra expenses to your life.

Well with direct sales I can figure out how much I want to make. I can give myself a raise or I can be broke and not make any money. The choice is mine and after figuring this out I chose to make more money!

I like sharing with my team how to do so and anyone else that is interested in advancing in their own business. This is one of the reasons for writing this book. I want to share with as many people as I can that no matter your circumstances there is a way to be successful. Once you can come to terms with the handicaps in your life that may hold you back which are any life happenings that come in to play you will be ready to take the world by storm.

Say you have no car, or maybe you just don't drive. I also know some very successful people that have health issues that make it even harder to get out and meet people. Well this may make building a business harder but not impossible. Especially now with Social Media and the way people can communicate just by having a smart device. And asking people for help is another way to get out and work your business. I'm one who hates to ask for help, but I have learned to be successful you need to be humble. You need to ask for help, you need to be open to learning and willing to try anything. Helpers can be a game changer if you need extra help as well. And the power of the phone is another tool that I feel is not used the way it could be.

A great example of this is a story I like to share that one of my representatives on my team used. She was in an abusive relationship and had a few kids. Wanting so much to make her own money so she can eventually make a change she had a very hard time getting out and about. They had one car and it was only available to her on 1 or 2 days a week. She used the car to take her young children to their doctor appts during the week when they had them or do the shopping etc.

Knowing this she had to plan strategically to get customers. So, if you can't go out and you can't canvas and talk to people the way we all normally try to do what other way can you get customers and make sales? Well this is where her planning was amazing. She used the good ole phone book and looked up all the doctor offices on her route. She called them and asked them if they would be interested in receiving a catalog and offered her products to them over the phone. Found out what the interest level was and got a contact person at each place.

When she was able to go out she took her brochures and dropped them off to every place that was interested and talked once again to the contact person. She let them know when she would be following up with them to get their orders, and they all were very excited about it.

I was completely amazed at her drive and persistence! There was no holding her back in making this work for her. She followed up with every single place she left books and was able to have an order that was over $800.00. This was possible by just using the phone and her transportation 1 day a week.

It proved to me that no matter what the circumstances are there is a way to make it happen if you want it bad enough. I share this story all the time because it's one that made a difference for me and for her.

Every book I read about success has one underlying theme, and that theme is hunger. How hungry are you to make it happen? What sacrifices are you willing to make to make it happen? How quickly do you want to make it happen?

This is what you need to ask yourself and this is what you need to start everyday out with! Remind yourself of your dream! And do something every day to get you one step closer to that dream! Set your goals, put together a plan, figure out what is holding you back and step outside of the comfort zone and every day you will get closer to achieving what it is that you set out to achieve.

Let's list some things that get in your way of being a success. Don't stop with that though, next to it write down how you can work to eliminate the problem:

~Setbacks~

"A setback is a setup for a comeback"

Setbacks in business and in life are part of the journey and this next chapter I really want to talk about how I made setbacks part of my success. I have covered many things so far and one thing about being part of direct sales for 17 years is that there are so many stories to share with each other that are not only life changing but business changing as well.

When I decided to join a direct sales company, I did some research first. I considered start up price and the value of what you get when you start. I considered how it needed to be sold, if there was inventory that you needed to have or buy. If you were required to do only home parties, if there was a minimum in sales required and if I was going to enjoy the products offered as well. There were a few that seemed like great choices, but it really came down to what was going to work for me. I also wanted to make sure that what I sold was consumable products so that my customers would always need to be re purchasing what it was they were getting.

I then made my choice and I said to myself that I was going to get started "as soon as" ... now this saying I hear still to this day when I'm out prospecting. I sat back for a few months before I finally made the call to get started. Yes, I procrastinated waiting for that perfect time just as many of you may have that are reading this now.

As I shared already this decision for me at the time was more of a hobby for a few years. I wasn't hungry yet and I really wasn't ready to take building a business seriously, but I did love the products and I enjoyed learning more about them and during this time I did complete a lot of the training and I put together a plan to take advantage of all that this company had to offer. I just didn't get moving on it very quickly. You see the one thing that I wish I had done more research on, would be a mentor. I really didn't know the value in having one when I got started nor did I think it was something I needed.

Well come to find out in direct sales like any business there are a bunch of mentors that you can choose to follow and get guidance from. Just like myself, giving back to others and helping them whether they are directly on my team or not because that is something other mentors did for me. This is how so much of my success grew and that was following some great mentors in the business! I learned that I didn't need an "immediate upline mentor" although that would've been nice from time to time but not necessary for success at all. Again, success is driven from within and no matter how great the people are around you if you're not willing to take what they have to offer and do something with it, it really does you no good.

The first thing I want to share that I learned from a mentor was the most important building block to any business and that is NEVER QUIT. You can slow down, you may even need to build some of your business while working another job. You may have life circumstances slow you down but if you don't QUIT you will always be moving forward even if that pace is slow and steady. Starting over really makes you feel like you are never going to get there.

Here is my story on never quitting. And I shared early about life circumstances that almost had me at the breaking point and quitting. I look at building a business like I would if I was a mountain climber. If we were to climb an enormous mountain, one that was going to take weeks to get to the top. Let's say we start the climb and it's easy, we are full of energy and ready to make it all the way to the top. Doesn't seem like anything can stop us because its new and we are ready!

A day or two on this climb we find that we have some blisters now. It has rained, and the wind is getting to you. Legs are starting to feel it and every step seems like it takes every ounce of energy to just lift the shoes. Feels like you're never going to make it to the top.

But it's been a few days and your almost ½ way there. So, you keep pushing. You may need to stop more to take a break, but you keep pushing.

Now it's been 4 days and you still can't see the top, your feeling like this was the worse decision ever and all you want to do is go home and sleep in your own bed, have a hot meal and get these shoes off your feet. I mean what were you thinking taking on such a mountain, others made it look so easy. Never thought it would be this hard and part of you wants to just turn around and call it quits. Now think about that, your better than half way or at least half way. If you turn around now you would have given up all that climbing, you already did. The view is amazing, and a helicopter will be picking you up at the top and the rewards are endless. Not many have made it to the top and it is a real dream you have. Are you willing to keep going? Maybe just set up camp and rest for a little longer right where you are. Re-evaluate your path and see if there is a less rocky way to go but you don't turn around and go home. You keep moving up that mountain because quitting and going down means that when you want to start this climb again you would've lost all the ground that you just covered. You will have to start from the bottom again. This is the importance of always moving forward. Always doing something to cover more ground upwards, towards that top where you are striving to be! That is the first and most important lesson especially in direct sales.

Now the second lesson I learned from a few of the mentors that I follow would be start one business, make it to the top of the pay plan before thinking you can start another one. I see so often so many people selling many different types of products and I never see them become successful in any one of them.

There is a reason and I want to share how I feel about it because it's important to understand what is happening if you are truly wanting to find success.

Ask yourself why you would want to split your efforts in ½ or in thirds? If you are looking for customers and you tell people you offer all these things, which company is going to be the one that makes you the most money? Now if you are just using direct sales to get a distributor discount than that's totally different. But if you're truly wanting to build a business then you need to be consistent to that one business and build it so that you are making money and once you are truly making enough money to sustain your lively hood now you can add another if you want to. Which truly isn't always a bad thing because many incomes are always better than just one.

The problem is, is that most people I have seen just jump from company to company and they never really give the first one a chance. They see what they think is a better opportunity and they run towards the new shiny toy. That toy becomes dull and stops squeaking and instead of shining it up and nurturing it they throw it aside and get the new shiny toy. No one will ever take you seriously in business, as a matter of fact they will just be sitting back waiting for you to join the next best thing.

You cannot build relationships this way, a team will never have confidence in you as a mentor and finding business partners will be very hard to do. I have found that in my business one thing I have started to hear a lot lately is "wow your still doing that direct sales business"? And it feels good to say, "yes I am" and it is an amazing opportunity that I would love to show you how to do the same. I have built credibility and loyalty to a brand and it is noticed especially with an online presence.

Now I have a few affiliate programs that I use in business that are not direct sales businesses they are tools I use and many of my partners use in business that helps them build the business they are in and while using these tools we earn commission on sharing it. Now this I look at as a smart way to pay for a service that you will be using anyways. That's called working smarter not harder.

If you are currently a distributor with several companies and you want to be successful and make good money in direct sales I would just simply suggest you pick one and make that the one you will be working. Keep the others if you use the products and enjoy a distributor discount but PROMOTE one of them. Work one of them and build one of them first! Pick the one that you know will make you the most money if you truly worked it as a business.

I get approached often from others in other direct sales businesses to "take a look" at their company. They tell me how wonderful it is and that I would make an amazing asset to their team. Well I have no doubt that I would, I see how much I have accomplished in my business that I work consistently. It is never good business to go looking at people in other sales organizations to join your team. This is tacky, and I lose a lot of respect for those that practice this within their business. Although it's a wonderful compliment, just ask yourself why anyone would want to quit their business that is doing great to start over?

And if they are with another company and struggling what makes you think business would be much better on a different team or even a different business? Usually people find success in having passion for what they do, that passion will drive them to success and beyond. That is what you look for when your prospecting, not someone who thinks it's their "upline" or company or products that are keeping them from making it.

Now a story I like to share with you about these two tips I just shared; I have had many, many bad days in business. Although none of my days have ever been bad enough to make me want to give it all up.

I sometimes feel like I should be so much farther ahead than I am then I look back at where I was when I started. It really brings so much to perspective. I really wish my mom would have lived to see the day I made the top level of the pay plan with my current direct sales company. Although I know she was there with me in spirit it would have been so great to share it with her in person.

Everything in my life up to then was against me in succeeding. My failed marriage was an obstacle, my mom's health didn't make it easy. I had zero family support and I honestly kept moving forward because I see the success in others that I wanted for myself. Looking back at the day I lost my mom reminds me all the time that once again I have chosen the right path! That morning I had my kids ready to go to orientation for school, my son Zack the oldest was entering middle school 6th grade so we needed to go see where his classes where.

I had all my deliveries in my trunk so that after we were done we were going to go make all my customer deliveries. It was beautiful outside, and it was exciting because just a few months prior to this day my divorce was finally finalized! So many things seemed like they were coming together at last. I had just returned for Las Vegas where we had attended the Leadership Convention for our company and so many positive things were about to happen. It really gives you the charge you need especially in direct sales.

As a matter of fact, I remember how broke I was on this trip, I had enough money for the airfare and the registration. The rest was living on a prayer, but we managed and made it happen.
My kids and I were walking up the stairs to get to the 6th grade hallway I received that phone call you pray you never get. My mom's oxygen guy was on the line telling me that he was at my mom's house and has called 911. He found her on the floor and she was unresponsive.

Honestly the rest of the morning is a bit of a blur, the school was right around the corner from my mom's, so we immediately turned around and headed back down the stairs to the car to hurry to my mom's. I just remember telling my kids we need to get to grandmas right away.

I talked to her the night before at 11:30 pm about my day and just like I always did I was planning on stopping there right after the orientation. I just couldn't imagine her being gone already. I ran into her house and I knew she was gone, and my life was about to change again in a matter of moments.

I'm sharing this story because like so many of you reading this, you have suffered lose and it seems so crippling at the time. Almost impossible to see the days later. If I had a job to go to I'm pretty sure I would've been fired between my divorce and all this. Most jobs don't give you as many days off as I would have taken, and they certainly don't pay you if you miss coming in.

I told you I had my trunk filled with deliveries for the day and all my customers where planning on me stopping. My friend called them all and explained and not one of those customers minded, as a matter of fact they were more than understanding as we rescheduled all them for the following week.

As life happens we need to be able to change with it and not let it drown us. It's easy to just quit and take the easy road, go get a job and collect a paycheck that will always just be a paycheck. It's easy to settle and become victim of circumstance, but to grow from it and let it be the fuel that helps you make that change is so much more powerful and the outcome is so much more rewarding.

I know my mom smiles at me all the time for not quitting, for always believing in myself and the opportunity that I have been able to turn into a success. I also love that I have shown my children how to overcome adversity and that with hard work you can accomplish whatever it is you want in life, no matter what life hands you.

As an only child there was no one to take care of things after my mom's death, only me. There were no extra people in my life to handle all the mess that followed for a few years that I never seen coming. All I do know is I didn't quit my business, I didn't put my business on hold for a year, so I can "get things done."

Imagine if the new department store that just opened down the road decided after being open for business a few years that they were going to "close up" for a while to take care of some personal business. I bet there would be no business when they returned. I'm not sure why so many treat their home-based businesses this way. They take off for all kinds of reasons, they take a "step back" they let me know that they will start selling again "just as soon as" and they give me their life reason why it just won't work right now.

Excuses, just excuses. That's what that is. Now you may not like hearing that, you may be ready to message me up and let me know just why this doesn't apply to you. Well I'm not here to judge, I'm only here to share my story, my experience and what has gotten in my way and how I managed to overcome and still make it. It may have takin me longer, but I continue to work on the growth.

Direct sales have no "salary cap" so why stop now, keep on growing and make even more money!

What are some setbacks? Write about them and find solutions to move forward.

~Planning~

"Plans are nothing;
Planning is everything"

Making and sticking to a plan is what this next chapter is all about. I found this to be one of the hardest things I had to learn with working from home. Many family members never took my home-based business seriously, probably because I wasn't taking it seriously. They needed me to run them places, watch their kids for them and many other volunteer tasks all because, well why not I'm home anyways right?

All seems fine and good for a while, until one day you look at your business and realize it's not going anywhere. Well it's not going anywhere because you're not working it. I would make a million excuses; the laundry needed done, the house needed cleaned, I needed to do x y and z with my kids because after all I'm home and I should be taking care of my family first, right? Oh, the best one is I started to take on tasks that if I was at a normal job I wouldn't be able to take them on. I got involved in PTA more, the church all sudden needed me to do phone calls and extra things from home. The sports my kids where in needed a secretary, the list was endless. I enjoyed these extra responsibilities because I was never able to do them before when working, there just wasn't any time. But these tasks were not making my house hold money, and my house hold was paying for my business. I added an extra expense and it was getting tough. I reached out to a mentor and explained my situation to her, she quickly made it very clear to me what needed to be done. I really didn't like the answer, but she was right, and I needed to take a good look at it and decide what I was going to do about my business.

She said, "Lisa do any of these tasks you're doing make you money?" well no they don't BUT I said, and she interrupted me with NO BUT! I then had to admit that no one was paying me to do laundry, or cook and clean, or make cupcakes for PTA or make phone calls for church etc. These are things that need to be done when I'm DONE working my business.

One of the best things about working your own business is that you can set your own schedule. But you must SET A SCHEDULE. That means the hours you put on your schedule for working your business need to just be for your business. Now like I discussed previously in this book, my business is a life style also so many times I can be working my business and running tasks like doctor appointments and grocery shopping, banking etc. But making phone calls, following up with customers and team members, attending meetings these things require my full attention and need to be done on a regular basis to be successful.

So, I did exactly that, I made a schedule just like I previously talked about. I put my kid's appointments down, I put other meetings down and I set aside the time I would be able to fulfill any obligation that didn't bring money into my household.

Now I was able to see the availability for my business. I could make good on being consistent. My customers got their deliveries on the day I promised. I had time set aside to contact team and return phone calls and emails etc. Every day I worked on my business, I did something that was going to help make me money.

People in my life started realizing that I took my business seriously and it made me feel good. I started learning how to SAY NO to the people in my life that clearly were taking advantage of me when it came to baby sitting and running them places or just plain volunteering me for activities that I clearly didn't always have time for.

And here is a story that I have heard time and time again in my business. It has happened unfortunately more than a dozen times on my own team, this doesn't even touch how many I see it on social media. It's the constant excuses for why we can't find success. They start a business and then take their kids out of day care or tell me that they can't find anyone to watch their kids a few hours a day, so they can work their business. They talk about how there is no extra money for sales tools and that they can't possibly invest even $10 extra dollars in brochures or samples to help them find customers.

All the while I see them buying purses or shoes or going to the movies. They may buy an overpriced coffee every time they leave the house, or they are out to dinner and fast food several times a week. They find a baby sitter to go to the bar with the friends or even a trip to the grocery store. But these same people won't watch their kids for them to make money with their business?

The sad part about these excuses is that their businesses fail. They don't make enough money to see the worth and many times they end up having to go "find a real job." My question to them is always the same "who is watching your kids." Your now gone 8-10 hours a day, you must have a certain wardrobe that may cost you money and you spend even more money "guilt shopping" for your kids because you don't see them nearly as much as you wanted to.

How did that help your situation? Well I have a story about this and how it made a difference in my business. Like I shared I started working at 15 ½ and I had one or two jobs consistently till I was laid off from my last job after having Zack. So being home was a HUGE adjustment for me and believe me as much as I loved being home it was hard at times to not have my own income. Now we did good as a family, our business that I helped my husband at the time build did well. I invested a lot of money into "our business" so he could do new trades and make more money. But he had no money management whatsoever. He spent more than he made, he didn't budget at all and he thought paying creditors was an option.

When I started my home-based business, as I shared, it was a hobby. I bought items we needed at home and gifts and things I liked for myself and my kids. The kids were so cute on delivery day because they thought it was always all for them, which a lot of times the majority was for them. My mom brought me some orders and a few friends ordered. It didn't change until I started leadership two years into my business.

I then started everything we have talked about. Customer searches were an everyday thing for me. I was digging right in. I started advertising which was costing me money the extra supplies cost me more money. I really wasn't using any profits on the house hold except for when my kids needed stuff. But I really didn't need to at the time either. We made plenty of money to pay the bills, and sometimes I paid my account with our other business checking.

One day my ex says to me "why are you always paying your account with the business money" and continued with "when will you start making money with that business." Well my blood boiled! I looked back on all the money I used when I was working sometimes two jobs to help him build his business. I thought about my severance pay I used to pay off debt he had accumulated with his spending habits, the extra time I put in helping him get to where he was in his business.

I promised myself at that moment, that "his business" will never spend another penny on mine! I made sure I reinvested every bit of what I made right back in and had even a stronger drive to make it a huge success.

I will admit that being able to just put back all my money into my business at that time really did help it grow much faster. And I had many team members and other associates that used to point it out to me on the regular that "I just don't understand how hard it is to have to try to live off this little bit of income." They were right, I had no idea because I never did it.

When my marriage came to an end my business almost did the same. It was amazing how many people on my team took me for granted. How much I did for them and at a time when I needed them most they quit! Not only did they quit some of them took their customers and gave them to other representatives. It really hurt to see just how many didn't stick with me. I realized I was carrying so many of them. So, when I couldn't carry them anymore they were gone.

My business took a big hit, I was on the brink of giving it all up. I shared earlier why I didn't do that. But it was hard, one of the hardest things I think I ever did. I was about 4 years into this business and 2 of them as you know I wasn't serious. So, all I had to really take a long hard look at where I needed to go from here.

When I share with you what works in business it's because I have done it, I had to do all of it. I have been on every end of the business spectrum. From not needing the money and using it to grow to needing every penny I made to survive.

After making the decision to stay and work my business and stay home with my kids at a time when they needed me most, I needed to learn and teach myself how to set these goals. Look at my customers, put together a plan and make action a daily part of my routine. I WAS HUNGRY. I WAS HUNGRY WITH A VENGANCE! I wanted to prove to myself first and then to my selfish ex, my family and to all the quitters on my team that I WAS A SUCCESS.

I'm still working on this every day, I make goals and I push myself harder than ever. I step outside my comfort zone and try new ideas and invest in new ways of making money and helping others. This is the beginning of my Success, the Success that has made life changes for me. Before we go on I want you to answer this next question.

Tell me what makes you HUNGRY?

~Adjusting Your "Sales" ~

"Make today the most productive day of your week"

Adjusting your "sales" is going to become something that you are going to have to do on a regular basis. With direct sales in any kind of businesses in general there are busy times and there are slower times. All the selling seasons need to be adjusted so that you continue to make the money that you want to make in your business. I want to take this chapter giving some ideas that have worked for myself and others during these different times of year.

The bestselling times for any business are a holiday. The Christmas season is the biggest, but there are other ones all year that are also great holidays that we can leverage to promote and increase our businesses. During the Christmas season whether you celebrate it or not, making money is making money. Don't miss out on the entire November till mid-January to increase your customers and sell more. A few things I love to do is offer specials such as "black Friday sales," giveaways, promotions and coupons. All reasons that will draw people to buy from you.

Don't stop with the day, make it a weekend and continue it to Cyber Monday! Another day to optimize sales to your web sites, most companies even offer discount codes and promotions that you can use as well.

How about a layaway event, make your own layaway plan for your customers to help them shop and spend more than they usually would have if they had more time to pay it off. Another wonderful idea to offer your customers is gift wrapping! You can either do it as a convenience for them or offer a small fee for the service, either way it's a great idea and you will be surprised how many people will take you up on it.

Watch other retailers and use the marketing that they use to keep your customers buying all month! I like to use a promotion for every dollar spent that earns a discount after the holiday. Be smart about having promotions, give a deadline and encourage your customers to come back to shop before the deadline expires.

Now November thru January does happen to be the biggest time of year to increase sales and that is why 4th quarter for most businesses is a huge time of year. So, what are other holidays and special calendar days and events that you can use to help promote your business and keep it growing?

February, I love to use Valentine's Day, the hallmark holiday that gives everyone a reason to buy something special for that someone special. This isn't just a couple's day, we also like to buy gifts for our children, our parents and now they even have school parties and other fun activities that you can use your business and your products to promote sales.

March, St. Patrick's Day is not usually one many people think about when it comes to getting sales or marketing their businesses, but why not! Have a shamrock party, use your brochure and hide shamrocks throughout it, if your customers find the shamrocks they get a special sample or a percentage off their next order. These types of fun activities are going to separate you from the other representatives selling products as well.

In April I like to use Uncle Sam as a reason to give a discount or offer a fun incentive for shopping. How about making it a great time to get people to join your team! Emphasize the fact that people with home-based businesses get to enjoy extra tax breaks that can help then when it comes to doing their taxes.

Sometime between April and May we have Easter/Passover or whatever it is you celebrate. I use Easter personally and start a week or so before using Plastic Easter eggs to hide special prizes and discounts. I love to carry a small basket around and offer them out to anyone I meet. It's a great conversation starter and everyone loves a surprise!

May is the month that Mother's Day falls into, which as we all know is all about making the moms in our life feel special. Watch the marketing here, it will mainly focus on the men and children that need to make mom feel special. I love to offer gift baskets this time of year. Although gift baskets are a great gift idea all year, most men love to buy a prepared gift. One that fits the budget they are looking for and it's all bundled up and ready to give. Be creative and offer a service that will not only get you repeat sales, but word of mouth will get you even more customers.

Following right into June is Father's Day. Now you may be thinking you don't have many things for the men, that your direct sales are primarily for women. But remember that there are a lot of women out there that are holding the mom and dad position in the house hold. I for one was raised with just my mom the second half of my life and I too ended up celebrating this with my kids as "the dad." Use this as a marketing tool and again get those sales! June is also the ½ way point to Christmas, so June 25th is exactly 6 months away and the countdown begins. People like to plan so put together something that can help them. Put together your Christmas In July open house. People are always looking for a great away to enjoy some refreshments and get together. A great way to talk about the upcoming Holiday and how you may even be able to help them start the year off making their own holiday cash with a homebased business.

July 4th is yet another Holiday that can "set sparks off in your sales." See how just a phrase can change how you view your business for a month. I love to use coloring sheets that customers can give their kids to color and turn back into me for a coloring contest. Pick the top three best ones and give away prizes to the winners, I usually give something to everyone who participates like a coupon off their next order.

August is a get ready for school month, between grade school, high school and even college parents are busy, and they are spending money on the kids. Unless your selling back to school items this month is a tough one, so you need to stand out and give your customers a reason to shop with you. Make it convenient and save them time going to the store for items they may need that you can offer them. It's also a good time to start letting them think about how an opportunity with you and your company can help make them some extra money or even save money when the kids are back in school.

September is all about focusing on the growth that you gained during the summer months. Think about all the new customers and team members that you gained during this time and follow up is going to be key. Even you will have more quality time to spend on your business now that your own kids are back to school. Start making your 4th quarter plan and revising your own schedule to create a more lucrative earnings opportunity. Plan some home parties or girl's nights that can help get everyone thinking about you and your business.

October is a fun month by far to be creative. Fall is beginning, and the weather is cooling off for many. Halloween or Harvest events will be going on at school and again whether you celebrate or not kids will be walking around your neighborhood or going to community events for tricks or treats. Look for "trunk n treat" events, many local churches and schools put these on to keep it fun and safe for the kids. I'm all about taking advantage any time of year where people are walking up to me or knocking on my door. Have your brochures ready and a nice "treat" for grown-ups that are walking with the kids. Get your information into as many hands as you can with little to no effort in doing so.

I need to touch on some fun stories about using every day happenings to help promote yourself. One of the biggest nuisances that I encounter is junk mail. Mail that I get that comes with a self-addressed envelope to send back to the marketer. Take these correspondences and put your information in them and mail them back in. It will cost you your time and a sample or whatever it is you want to send them. How about recruiting information or a link to shop with you online. And how about the people that knock on your door, they want you to buy something from them so why not use this opportunity to tell them about what you do and make sure they leave with your information as well. Even an occasional email can be responded to with your information. I feel that all these situations can lead to a prospect for you just the same, by using the time they spend in trying to get you to recognize them.

I have always loved the marketing part of my business, the chance to think outside the box and really use ideas to help me promote myself and business. From day one I enjoyed making flyers and coupons and different things to give to my customers to endorse my business. When you're just starting off there usually isn't a bunch of money to spend on advertising, so you need to be creative. And as you start to make more money you can venture into larger ideas.

My 1st serious year with my company was my 2nd year like I shared earlier on. I was an amazing personal shopper for my first two years, I wanted to have a homebased business, but I also knew that my business could grow slowly as my kids got older. My plan was by the time my son hit kindergarten, well it started earlier than that because my friend wanted to sell. Since I had taken all the training available I understood if I started leadership I was going to need to increase my sales.

The little bit of selling I was doing was fun, but I needed treat it a whole lot more serious to make it really work. I started looking in the paper and found every single craft show in my area. I contacted them and locked myself into participating in them. I put together a plan to book an event every weekend. I started to invest in inventory, so I would be able to have some success. I also turned my garage (which was attached to my house at the time and heated) into a small store for the holidays. This really helped not only increase my sales, but I found a bunch of customers.

Every event I did I had a giveaway, so I could collect names and numbers of everyone who stopped by my table. I offered samples and brochures, but the most important thing I did was get follow up information. Follow up information is where the repeat sales come from. Not only did I make the second level of sales achievement with my company I also had the largest increase of over $15,000 which also earned me a trip like I shared earlier and an award at our banquet. I was super excited of my growth in a short time and it proved that when I committed and took my business seriously I would see growth and more money.

Another excellent tip I share is to increase brochures when you order. I always made sure I have an extra hundred brochures to pass out every two weeks. This is key to growth and helps to keep you committed to working a consistent business. I still follow these same rules in my business. I may give the brochures out differently now, but I still make that investment for growth, I mean why stop now? There is no cap on what we can be paying ourselves so I'm all for making as much money as I can.

I have shared a lot of my marketing ideas here in this chapter that have worked and still work for me. At the end of this book you will find some of the ideas shared here like the coloring page, fundraising ideas, coupons and other miscellaneous marketing tools that work. Feel free to do similar things to promote and "adjust your sales" as the months change. Many of my ideas are far from unique but that is just another beautiful thing about networking. You can get ideas from other home-based business owners and use them with yours.

Now take a moment and write down what you want to use to help your business grow, add some of even your own ideas that I haven't mentioned:

~Prospecting~

"You don't have to be great to start, but you have to start to be great"

Prospecting is the biggest question in direct sales that I personally get on a regular basis. That being said let's start by sharing that this takes practice. I get so annoyed when I see advertising on social media from marketers that want you to think that it just happens overnight. It doesn't really happen overnight. It takes time and persistence. Not being pushy but by building relationships with people everywhere you go. Sharing your story, sharing why you do what you do and fitting it into their lives and showing them how to use your opportunity to make a goal or dream a reality with not adding more to their already busy schedule.

Sounds impossible?? Not at all and hopefully after reading some of this you will be on your way to prospecting all the time. Best story shared is how shy we are when we start off, I know believe it or not I was a bit shy when I first started my business. I hated pressure and didn't believe in confronting people with anything especially a business opportunity.

Things that hold us back are the same across the board. We don't see the money yet in our own business so it's hard to share it with someone else. We are new and not real sure how to do it or what to say or how to train them if we get them to join. Among other things these are the easiest to fix. I want to share more about my very first recruit and how I kept recruiting more people after that first one.

When I started I was a personal shopper, like I shared this was a business I was working on slowly, it wasn't a need of mine it was just a want and there is a big difference in the two. When a friend of mine inquired about it I was excited, and I thought "oh no" basically because I knew she really needed the money. I shared with her how I was making a little money but that I also met a lot of people that were very successful in it. I also assured her that we would work together on building customers and growing together as a team.

I'm a competitive person and I compete with myself more than I do with others, so as soon as she started I was able to look at the compensation plan my company offered and the bonuses I could earn. I immediately shifted my business into full gear. I had two small children and a household to run, I also had a mind that was buzzing with ideas and I wanted it all.

The first thing I decided to do was start advertising in our local paper, which now in days isn't the best option because most people don't read the paper. But back then they did, and I knew I could get some "warm" prospects from doing this. I did get calls and some of them worked out. It gave me the opportunity to learn how to talk about the business and learn from my mistakes. I bought some books from other direct sellers and leadership people, so I could get some ideas on how to continue to grow, and that really helped as well.

I quickly started to see some growth and I started to earn a small amount of money. Back then everything was done face to face. There was no networking online, so everything was done personally. This is still a very good way to build a strong foundation. Putting my brochures everywhere all the time. Handing them out to people in person and getting names and numbers at events was were my biggest success came from. The fortune is in the Follow UP.

Building a strong team means you have a strong foundation. It is no different than building a house. If your foundation is weak your house may fall, and while I was building my foundation, like I shared earlier some of my "bricks" where very weak and I had to continually add more "mortar" to them to keep them strong. This is time consuming and as I learned later eventually they crumble regardless. You always need to be adding stronger "bricks."

I love building relationships and adding to my team, it's very rewarding to see someone build on their dream and achieving what they want. As time went by times changed and so did the way I did business. It became harder to place ads as the internet started up. We direct sellers were stuck between the old way and the new and upcoming way of doing business and this took some time and adjusting to finally get totally transferred over. Fast forwarding to the more current time we have wonderful tools at our disposal like Face Book, Instagram, Pinterest, Twitter, Google Plus and many more simple apps like Next Door and selling groups. It's a whole new world.

This new world I think sometimes makes it harder to do business, I feel that many people get stuck thinking that putting up posts or blogs are going to get them where they want in business. Well it takes more than that, I personally have success in a lot of the old ways of doing business with a splash of networking. It's a nice combination of both that will show you growth much quicker than just waiting for someone to show interest in your online post. If you have time to spend and money isn't something you're looking to make right away, then just working on selling online is probably a good fit. I believe that relationships are the fastest way to a successful recruiting business.

A fun tool that was introduced to me and others that works with prospecting is something called a "try it kit." It is a simple way of putting a few items together for prospects that won't cost them a dime to try your business. We include a few brochures, an order book with a couple samples in a small bag and an introduction sheet. All the prospect needs to do is take the brochures around to some friends and family and see if they can collect orders. Give them a small goal to reach and if they can reach that goal then they are more likely to join up and be off to a great start.

Give the prospect a week or so to collect customers and orders, meet back up with them and see how it went. If it goes well then have them start up immediately and place those orders. Showing them how easy it is to make some extra money without a huge commitment, it's a concrete plan for recruiting.

Another fabulous way to recruit is to convert customers over to team members. I love this way because most of the time your customer already loves your products. Here is my tip, when invoicing them, invoice them twice. Once with the total they need to pay and one more time including the discount they would receive from being a representative.

Everyone loves a discount and I can say from experience this works just about every time, they see that savings and jump on board. One of the first customers I converted over to join my team was a consistent customer. I hated to recruit her or any of my customers because at the time I was still building a customer base. All I could think about at the time was the fact that I was losing a good order. Well much to my surprise that customer that ordered approximately $25.00 to $40.00 every two weeks started placing orders on her own for over $300.00. I remember calling her and congratulating her on her success and asked her how she was doing it. Her response was that she brought some brochures to her job and all her coworkers were ordering. I thought to myself at the time how funny it was that when she was just a customer she never got any additional orders for me. Not that I was going to complain but it proved the point that we work harder for ourselves than we ever would for someone else. My recruit was earning enough extra cash to help pay for her own stuff as well as surprise expenses that popped up in her house hold.

There are a lot of different ways to market yourself and get your business in front of new people all the time. Use your imagination, copy what other retailers do and leave the fear of success at the door. Don't hold back, be confident in what you do, and others will follow that. Haven't you ever heard the saying money follows money? Well success will follow success. Just be the person you would want to follow and believe me everything else will fall into place.

I talked about prospecting here, shared some ideas. Take a moment and write down what you thought about. Put your thoughts into action!

~Leadership~
"Be the leader YOU would follow"

Leadership and being a good leader are to entirely different things. Since I started my business with no immediate upline I really had no idea what to do with a team of representatives to train and lead. I took a lot of tips from other mentors and I started off doing things for my team that I would have loved to be part of if I myself was part of someone else's team. Even if you are part of someone's team, you need to be asking yourself if you're doing all you can do to be a positive and strong leader for your own leg of the business.

The first thing I started to do from day one was put together a nice bi-weekly newsletter. My team at the time was all local so we could have local meetings together and other types of get togethers. I did recognition for them and gave small gifts away for their performance. We worked together on reaching incentives that the company put on as well, because why not take advantage of everything available for growth.

I didn't spend a lot of money on any of this at first because you need to make whatever you do duplicable for your team members so that if they are interested in building a team they will be able to do the same with little to no extra money or experience. This is when it's so very important to lead by example.

Since there was no internet when I started in leadership we did everything via email or "snail mail" we also relied a lot on local meetings to learn and share about business. I have seen now with the way times have changed and the big ole web that this has made some of these things easier and some of it harder on us.

Don't just rely on Facebook or email or text messaging for building a relationship with your team. Now I realize there are some people you will just never get on the phone. But don't let that stop you from trying. If texting is the way people want to communicate then by all means text them. Some people only like emails and others really do like to communicate via phone. You need to be willing to do all the above.

You also need to be consistent. I say this quite a bit throughout this book, but it really is one of the keys to success. Right up there with follow up. If you start doing a bi monthly newsletter with recognition be sure you do it consistently. Don't just start it up and then stop. It looks bad and will make it hard to start back up. Set the day of the week or month that you want to put it together and mark that down on your calendar. Also, if you want to do training meetings and you have a team like myself now that isn't just local it's all over the United States, meeting in person is probably not going to happen. You will need to look up free tools to use as a group like freeconferencecall.com or zoom. Maybe you have another service that you can use for free that can be used by groups of people. Now plan a regular meeting and repeat that day and time so people can mark their calendars and plan on attending. For the team members that can't attend be sure you have a recording to share with them, so they don't miss out. It will also keep them interested and in the future make them want to try and make it live.

Social media has made keeping in touch with most people easy, but you are always going to have team members that don't want to be on the computer for any kind of reason, especially if their "full time" job requires that of them. Be sure you make accommodations for all. It's your job as a leader to LEAD. Be that example that you have always wanted to follow.

I try to do as much as I can for my entire team and all my leaders. Not everyone does this, and I guess it really is their choice since it's their business. But if I have leaders on my team that can't or don't want to train or do meetings and trainings and recognition I'm right here to pick up the slack. After all their team is part of my team so regardless of where they are placed I want to make sure they get the help and training they need.

I love watching my team grow and I also love helping the team members on my team that want more out of their businesses. I have learned however that it's not for everyone. Some people have joined our company for just the discount, they fall into that "personal shopper" category. Others may really love their career choice and only wanted to have an account, so they can get a discount and offer it at work to make a little bit of extra money. Then I have those that join because they really want a home-based business and they work hard to make all those dreams they have a reality. You need to be flexible and you need to know what it is they want. No one likes a pushy leader.

Other representatives in the company I'm in now and other companies have reached on occasion to me to complain about the lack of help they receive from their immediate upline in their business. Or they share that because they are not interested in leadership themselves they have been told they don't really have much help for them, almost like pushing them off because they are not that important to their growth. Well this is terrible business, and I'm here to share that if you have had that said to you or if you have said that or given that impression to someone on your team, that it's terrible. But at the end of the day as I have shared before, this is your business. Your up line will not make or break your business. They can enhance it, but they can't break it. Step up your own game and again be the leader you would want to have.

Have incentives for your team the same way you have them for your customers. Share what is working in your business and help them to add more value to their own businesses. Whether you have one or two members or one hundred to thousand or more team members. Work it strong, be consistent and lead by example. I for one have never asked or told any of my team to do something that I don't currently do or have done. I show them that I work just as hard still today as I have from the day I took my business seriously.

Another thing is never pre-judge, you just never know what someone is going to do with their business. Look at me for example,

I was a personal shopper when I started. Who would ever have thought that I would have made this business a multimillion-dollar business. Our lives can change at any moment, again another reason to always have that back up plan. Home-based businesses make a great back up plan.

My favorite recruiting story is one that proves persistence. As I shared when I first started my business times were different and most of my prospects came from putting ads in the local paper. I did this every Sunday consistently for a few years. Like clockwork my ad would show up under help wanted and people would call, not all of them were serious and many stood me up, but I did get growth ongoing along with all my other efforts in finding prospects.

I had a woman call me on this one Sunday that had seen the ad, I want to share this story because this same representative is still part of my team. She has stuck with her business all these years later. When I spoke to her on the phone and set up the appointment I knew she was a little bit older than me and not the normal "I need a job type of call." I set up an appointment to go to her home and when I showed up she had a beautiful home set up with some of her other family. She was an educated woman that had a full-time job. She was interested in our business because she loves the products and wanted to make extra money. When talking with her I learned that she had been seeing my ad in the paper for a long time, probably over a year. One day she read an article about the company in one of her magazines and that was the moment she decided to call me. She called ME because she seen the ad for so long and felt like it was a sign that she should act on her impulse to start up.

Now this is a great example of persistence. Doing things in your business consistently all the time that gets your name out there and letting people see it repeatedly. It works, and this was just what I needed as proof.

Use every tool you can to promote yourself and your business. Not just one here and there, all of them all the time. Take it seriously and let others know you are in this for the long haul. Share your growth, everything you accomplish should be a celebration and you need to make it just that.

Take a few minutes, write down what you use to promote yourself and add other ideas if you have them while you're at it:

~Making it a Family Business~

"Make it a family business."

My favorite reason for loving home-based businesses so much is the fact that you can include your family in it and enjoy not only making money but doing it with your kids, husband, wife or significant other. Since my children were so small when I got started, I worked my business mainly when they napped or went to bed. They had very good schedules and this made it easy to spend some time on calls and training. During the day I enjoyed taking them with me to do book drops and deliveries. I was able to spend quality time with my mom as well. She would come over early and drive around with us, like a big fun family event.

It was great having the support of my mom because she was able to come over early and help me not only with the kids but with separating my orders and preparing brochures for our outings. My husband then really didn't involve himself with my business although he did silently support it in his own kind of way. I learned since my divorce that having someone in your life that really supports your business and helps you along makes a bit of a difference, but I was able to find success with both because I chose to and had a goal that I wanted to achieve.

Having my kids involved was a great way for them to earn little presents. Whether it was a McDonalds toy for lunch or a quick stop to the Dollar Store for something, they were able to at least see the value in working with Mom and I loved always having them with me. I truly loved staying home with them and being there for all the firsts that they had to encounter.

Being home with them and really learning how to schedule your work at home and your home-based business does require some discipline though. You need to stick to the schedule, a bed time was never a choice, it was necessary and when your home you can stick with that schedule. As they grew so did my business. When they started school, I was able to incorporate more day time activities it really was the perfect situation. I had a nice business going when I had found out I was pregnant with my third child John. This is where making it a family business really took on a whole new meaning.

It seemed anytime in my life when I felt I had things all figured out something would happen life changing that altered the course somehow. And this pregnancy was no different. My son Zack was almost 7 and my daughter Mikayla was just turning 5 and going into kindergarten, which I was super excited about. Since finally both kids were going to be in school all day, however I did have both in preschool at 3, but that was only ½ day and I used my earnings from my business to pay for that and for any extracurricular activities they got involved in.

I had moved up with my business and was about to achieve the top selling leadership level and my sales were amazing. I had a huge customer base to take care of and my plan that my business would grow as my kids did was going just the way I wanted. Imagine my surprise when I found out about the new baby on its way, this was not in my plans. I do love that saying, you may have heard it before "if you want to make god laugh, tell him your plans." Another reason I was upset about another baby was I could see my marriage heading in a direction that might not support another child, and it was heart breaking.

Well moving forward, I had a beautiful baby boy, this is when John came into the picture. He was more than life changing and for a couple of months I thought John may even save the marriage. We made a few life changes and during this time is when my husband decided to be unfaithful. This is an absolute deal breaker for me, and this is when my life took a much different path as I shared in the first part of the book.

John was a little over one years old and my other children where 6 and 8. This event changed the course of everything I had started. Now I shared part of this story already. But what I didn't share was how I needed to make different changes with my kids and my business moving forward.

It was nice that the older two where in school all day but now not only was my marriage over, my business was falling apart at the same time. I needed to literally start over rebuilding my business and I had to do it with a kid in tow as well. I was able to get him in day care/ preschool a few days a week for a few hours, so I could do appointments and attend meetings. It was hard to do this because I had never put my other two kids in any kind of day care when they were as small as John. But again, when your trying to build a business you need to make sacrifices to make that happen.

My mom's health wasn't well enough to baby sit or travel around with me now but again as a firm believe that god has a plan people stepped up and into my life that made a huge impact and difference in my life and business.

Now I know he isn't going to want me to mention his name in this book, but this person made a significant impact in my life, my business and my future. When someone comes along when you least expect it and steps up to help you stay as focused as they can and pick up with things that need done as they come up, that's a blessing that I can never be over looked. To be honest I would have never in a million years had thought that this person would've been the person they are today to me. He not only changed my grim circumstances but altered my future and my business as well.

Moving into how my kids make a difference in my business. John being the youngest has been part of my business his entire life. He only knows his mom as the "work at home mom," even though my older two children were basically raised with it as well, the age gap keeps him around me more while my older two were busy with sports and school activities.

This brings us to the current situation and how exciting it is to have a successful home-based business. My older children are now in college and John is still in middle school. We decided to have him attend online school, so we can travel together and attend trips and events that are many times out of town. I'm very excited about this opportunity and I would never have had it if I would have quit at any time during the challenging times in my life.

Get your children involved with your business as much as you can, it is, after all, a legacy you can leave for them once you build it up big and strong. Even if you don't think they will want to take it over in the future, as an MLM the residual income would make a difference in their life for quite some time.

When I was new to the business all my friends were starting jobs and families. I heard how they were all considering college funds and things to have for their children when they were ready to go off to college. I never really worried about it and my goal has been and still is, to let my kids learn how to get themselves through college. I feel that if they work for scholarships and grants take out loans when necessary, this will teach them a bit more about life and give them the satisfaction of earning their education and not having anything handed to them. After all no one handed anything to me my entire life. I worked hard for everything I had and have today, and I really love the fact that I can look back and see all that I have accomplished on my own. Now financially I help my children in other ways, I was able to buy both my older kids their first cars. Used a bonus for my sons and took out a loan for my daughters. I did this for my daughter because she wanted a newer car and wanted to help towards paying for it. It feels good to be able to do those types of things without worrying if we can afford it. I do however have them both pay for their own gas and insurance, I feel it's a responsibility that is important to learn as soon as you want to drive. Both kids started a part time job at 16. I don't believe in handing my kids anything, I do believe in showing them the value of money and working hard in life, after all I won't be here forever, and I need to be sure they can survive when they grow up and live on their own.

My college plan for my children is to be making even more money by the time they graduate. I will at that point help them to pay off any debt they have if they finish school and get a job. That to me is a solid plan to help them build a nice future.

Looking at your situation whether you younger starting out or starting out later in life, there is always family that you can involve in your business. Some of my close friends and team members have grand children or nieces and nephews that help them with their businesses. The beauty of being your own boss is the freedom to include who you want and work with who you love to work with.

How does your business involve your family? What ideas might you incorporate moving forward?

~Fundraising~

"Small actions times a lot of people equals big change"

Fundraising is the easiest and by far the most profitable way to not only earn money but find new customers and recruits all while helping another organization reach a goal financially. I find that a large percentage of people do not take advantage of this opportunity, primarily because they don't know how to get started.

I love finding organizations that are looking to make some money. Let me start by giving you a few ideas that you see every day in your normal life. First one is the car washes that especially during the warmer months, school clubs and sports teams will be outside washing cars for $5 or $10 dollars. It's hard work and they really don't make much money. Stop by and get your car washed, talk to the person in charge and make a small presentation on your fundraising opportunity. Get their follow up information and set an appointment up with them while your there to sit down and show them how you can help them earn the money they need in a much shorter time.

How about the people in a time of need, all over social media you will see go fund me accounts or benefit dinners/events that someone you know or someone you know may know and they shared the information. Take a moment and reach out personally to those people. Offer them an opportunity to earn the cash, at least with a fundraiser you have products that they are offering to the people that are helping them out. It's a win for everyone.

Schools are harder to get but once you get in I guarantee you will probably have a repeat customer year after year. Preschools are fun and so are daycares and since they are usually privately owned they are much easier to work with and more likely to participate.

Sports are another fabulous group to target. I know with my three kid's year after year they need to buy sports gear or pay for travel or new equipment. By showing them as a group how they can profit off your products while doing little to no work with a turnover in just a few weeks makes it hard to say no.

Now that you have a concrete lead that wants to do a fundraiser I want you to make it a success for you and the organization. The best way to do this is by planning for them. Set a goal, use the amount of people that are participating and an average according to what they will be selling. Break it down by person on how much they need to sell. Don't just hand them material and count on them to do it themselves. If you can once you have this prepared set a meeting with the entire group. Show them the presentation and share with them their individual goals. If these individual goals are met the group will together meet the main objective and everyone will come out a winner!

I like to offer prizes for the top sellers. This gives them even more motivation to go out and crush the goal, we all know everyone loves to win prizes. Remember you are your own boss and you get to set the earnings that you want to give to the organization. Do what works for you and them, make it so that they tell everyone they know how well it went because word of mouth is going to work in your favor big time here.

Now don't just do the fundraiser and end it without using your wonderful business experience in finding new customers. Be sure that you give every single person a thank you note with your name and information on it. Ask them to share your information with anyone who may be looking for a representative or another fundraising opportunity. Also, be sure to tell everyone how it went. Use your social media to promote yourself and share how wonderful the fundraiser went, don't hold back because this will get you a few referrals and possibly a few prospects too.

Fundraising is more work than just selling and you will need to really be organized to pull off a big fundraiser off with success. More people should take advantage of the money they can earn as well as the people they could be helping along the way.

One of the first fundraisers I did was for a small dance studio. I was new at everything and really had no idea what I was doing. I let them pick their flyer and really didn't put together a plan. The fundraiser still went ok, but it was a good learning experience for me. One little girl did pretty much all the selling and I did reward her for it. But I feel like if I would have had a little bit more direction I really could have helped them make more than they did. The following year they contacted me again. I was surprised, especially since I didn't think it went as good as it should have. But they called, and I was ready to do it again and do it better. Believe me it went better than the first time and because I had some experience I was able to offer more to them the second time around. They did great and I felt a whole lot better when it was finished. Since then I have always picked up smaller groups which is ok for the volume I do in just customer sales, but I have several friends and team members that do very successful fundraisers every year that not only help to build their businesses, but they reach higher sales levels by continuing to pursue them.

What are the organizations in your area that could benefit from a fundraiser? Take a few minutes and write them down.

~Success~

"Success is not the key to happiness,
Happiness is the key to Success"

Success is our goal when wanting to start any kind of venture in life. Whether it be education, relationships, careers or our own businesses we all strive to be successful. It really doesn't matter what it is, I believe starting out that, that is the plan, the plan to make it a Success. What happens once we get on a path is an entirely different thing. Everyone views failures a little different in life. I don't believe that anything is ever a complete failure. I believe we have lessons that we need to learn in life as we go no matter what it is that happens, if we learn from it and become a stronger, better person we can use it as a tool to be better tomorrow.

My youth taught me how to grow up and take responsibility for my life earlier than most of my friends. My marriage gave me 3 amazingly beautiful children to share my life with and although the marriage didn't last, I would never change the experience it taught me. Losing my mother before I was even 40 and my kids were young I thought was a punishment, but I know she is with me still every day.

I was given an opportunity to be reunited with my ½ sister Robin about the same time I was going through my divorce. You see, I got again, exactly what I needed in my life to move forward. We both get mad that we missed so much of each other's lives, but we also know we were brought together at the exact time we were going to need each other the most.

The many jobs that I had were all a stepping stones to teach me tools that would help me in my business and the ups and downs in my life and business have helped me to work harder than I ever would have if I didn't have them at all. I'm thankful for the trials in my life, without them I would never have become the person I am today. It's hard to see the silver lining in the clouds while its storming outside but once the sun comes out not only can you see the lining but if you're lucky you may even see a rainbow.

It doesn't matter where you are in your life right now, your age doesn't matter, where you are in your business doesn't matter and whatever it is that is going on in your life really doesn't matter. What matters is what you do with it today, tomorrow and the next day. We can't change our past, we can only work to build a better future. Nothing happens overnight, and it takes time to heal from hurt and it takes time to build a business. Life is a learning opportunity to make the best of while you're learning how to live. Sounds funny but believe me no one has it all figured out. Everyone has a story, and everyone must start by learning how to walk. I was told one time that while I had and still have so many people that I look up to and want to be like, even those people put their pants on one leg at a time. So, don't think for one second that you're not smart enough, good looking enough or lucky enough to be Successful. I'm here to share that you don't have to be anything special to live your dreams and luck has nothing at all to do with Success. All you need to be is willing enough to do whatever it takes to make it happen.

Learn that what you put out into the world you will get back. Although I used to feel like I really must had done something terrible in a past life to constantly have what I thought was "bad" things happening to me all the time. I felt like damn, I'm never going to catch a break, then when I did catch a break something else was waiting right around the corner to smack me in the head. This was not bad luck, this was and continues to be life.

Everyone has "stuff" and we all are given the same air to breathe. Stop making excuses and plan. Stop looking for the easy road and bust your butt to make things happen. Go around some of those road blocks and the ones that stop you dead in your tracks, I want you to stop, learn from it and then move it out of your way. Have you ever heard the saying "entrepreneurs and self-employed people will quit a 40 hour a week job to work 80 hours a week for themselves"? Well it's true, I know I work harder for me than I ever would for someone else, and the rewards I get are well worth every bit of it too.

Now it's time to dig in, take what you like from this book and leave the rest. This is my story that I like to share, and if it helps just one person then it has accomplished exactly what I intended when writing it. I truly love to share Success stories and help others grow and get outside of their comfort zones. The beauty of home-based businesses is that so many of us have so much in common.

Wishing you all the Success there is! Reach for the stars and never stop believing in the dreams that keep you moving forward.

Your Resources for Adjusting Your Sales

As mentioned in my Chapter "Adjusting you Sales" here are the marketing flyers I use. Make them your own, personalize them and be creative. Remember these are just my ideas and this gives you a visual of how to put together some great marketing ideas.

Other things I've used as contests with customers are word searches and puzzles which can all be done very easily on google for free, just google coloring pages, word search puzzles etc.

Remember being your own boss and having the ability to use all your own creative energy is just one of the amazing perks to having your own home-based business!

COLORING CONTEST

Color picture – Mail back by mm/dd/yyyy

Prizes
1st prize
2nd prize
3rd prize
Mail to: Your name: your address
COUPON FOR MOMS!! Place an order by mm/dd and save $5.00 OFF a $25.00 order!

Name:
Address:
Email:
Phone:
Age of Child coloring picture:

FUNDRAISER
EARN MONEY FOR YOUR GROUP IN 2 WEEKS!!

15 people each sell to at least 10 friends and family
Minimum one item off sheet *(products we use every day)*
Your GROUP WILL EARN $787.00

20 people do the same
Your GROUP WILL EARN $1,050.00

I will be more than happy to help you achieve your
GROUP GOALS!

(Your Company) And something that makes the fundraiser with
you different.

This will require everyone to participate and I will
be here every step of the way!
Let's plan a sit-down meeting to go over all the
details and get you and your organization the
money you need right away.

Your name
Title
email
Phone

EARN MONEY FOR YOU ORGANIZATION IN JUST TWO WEEKS!!

If your group has 15 people, in two weeks you could have as much as $787.50

If your group has 20 people, in two weeks you could have as much as $1.050.00

Here is a simple breakdown of how it works and how you can explain it to the group. Use the second sheet to carry around with you and to pass out to the organization you would like to have the fundraiser with.

This is figuring the organization out at a 35% profit -
15 people each sell to 10 friends and family – a minimum of $15.00 to each one is $150.00 order goal.
15 x $150.00 = $2,250.00

(That's 50% earnings for you!!)
Offering 35% to an organization is a good profit. You can give them more just rework the figures.
The Group will earn $787.50

You will earn $337.50 – a nice bit of change for not having to do much ;) now you work your magic and turn **these new orders into customers** – the **sellers into representatives**! Show them how they can do this themselves for their group next time!!

20 people each sell to 10 friends and family – a minimum of $15.00 to each
20 x $150.00 = $3,000.00

(You earn of course 50%)
**offering 35% to the organization
The Group will earn $1,050.00

You will earn $450.00! – So, in two weeks the group can earn $1,050.00 and you can earn $450.00 for motivating them!

You can rework this on the percentages or the amount of people – You want to show them the money!! Offer a prize for the one who sells the most – this is a GOAL FOR THEM! They can easily exceed this goal and do even more! Encourage them to exceed it!

The key to fundraising is to get them ALL ENGAGED! Help them get the money they need to get what they want and to have fun doing it! Watch the training videos in pathways and just be prepared.

Attached is a form that I like to type out just for them to look at with some fundraising flyers.

- Be creative with a prize for top achievers
- Be enthusiastic
- Stay organized
- Keep in constant contact with the person in charge
- Be professional

Thank you so much for your _____ donation for the **RORY THE LION** Fundraiser that will help to support

_____.

Thank you so much for your _____ donation for the **RORY THE LION** Fundraiser that will help to support

$5.00 GIFT CERTIFICATE

Presented to A NEW CUSTOMER

This certificate entitles the bearer to $5.00 off a $25.00 purchase.

$5.00   *Call*   *to redeem*

GIFT CERTIFICATE

Presented to A NEW CUSTOMER

This certificate entitles the bearer to $5.00 off a $25.00 purchase.

$5.00   *Call*   *to redeem*

LAYAWAY FOR THE HOLIDAYS

SHOP NOW… PAY AS YOU GO AND GET ALL THOSE MUST HAVE GIFTS FOR YOU LOVED ONES! HERE IS HOW IT WORKS:

1. Shop in the Catalog
2. Make a list here on the attached sheet
3. I will total the order and you need to pay at least _____%
4. The remainder will be divided into 4 payments of _____
5. Gift wrapping is available upon request

Guidelines of my Holiday Layaway

- There is no cash refund
- If you decide you don't want the layaway I will figure out products that have been paid for and give you those items that add up to the amount paid
- All sales are final, we only have a 90-day return policy, and this will exceed that
- If you miss a payment I will have to sell remainder items and give you what has been paid for
- You will receive the products when last payment is made

In signing this you agree to my terms of the Layaway
_____ Date _____

Start date of Layaway _____
Amount deposited _____

1st payment _____amount _____ Initials _____
2nd payment_____ amount_____ Initials _____
3rd payment _____amount _____ Initials _____
4th payment_____ amount_____ Initials _____

Special Thanks...

There have been people in my life that have supported me, continue to support me and have held me up along my way.

First and foremost, I want to thank my biggest mentor and now friend - Lisa "Captain Platinum" Wilber, she has paved a path of success that I have wanted since the first time I heard her story. Her marketing genius and determination is one that I admire. From day one if it worked for Lisa I knew I needed to do it.

I also want to thank my manager Anita Traylor, she was the first person I met in my business and when I needed her she was there, without an upline Anita became more than a manager, she became part of my family and I love her for that. I was lucky enough to have her as part of my business for the entire time our company had managers. Thank you so much for your constant inspiration!

A heartfelt thank you to the man that has been by my side through the hardest parts of my life, then stayed to celebrate the triumphs as well. I believe that God has a plan and that everything happens for a reason, and you are one of the best unplanned gifts that I could have ever received. Thank you, Eric Mullins, for loving me no matter what, and for holding me up when I couldn't hold up myself.

I want to thank my customers; a good portion of my customers have been with me since the beginning of my direct sales career. Through all my trials and tribulations of life, they have stood by me and watch my business grow. They have been part of my success and I will always be grateful for them.

I need to give a big shout out to my TEAM! Without my team there really would be NO Success. My team is what drives me to be a better person every day. They give me the ambition to jump out of bed and get started every morning. I love watching them grow and get closer to their own dreams. My team is my foundation and I love that I have been blessed to have them as part of my business. They make me want to be the best I can ever be.

My Direct Sales family, the people that have been added to my life because of my Direct Sales career. Many of my closest friends have been introduced to me through my business and I know will be with me the rest of my life. You know who you are, and I want to thank you for being the family that I've needed. Thank you for all your love and support, not only in business but in my life.

For being one of the "Formidable Four," the start of an amazing journey that not only helped me step out of my comfort zone but has created a wonderful pallet of learning for all representatives. The opportunity to share without drama with each of us contributing our strengths to help others in achieving Success. Lisa Wilber, Molly Stone-Bibb and Theresa Paul, I love you all.

My inspiration for wanting to get my book translated to Spanish goes to my "bestie" Jeanpierre Bongiovi. JP your such an amazing example of what hard work and dedication can do if you stay focused and work hard. I'm so happy our businesses brought us together -I just love you.

Lots of love to my sister Robin Scola, although we missed a huge portion of our lives together, having you in my life these past several years have more than made up for any time we missed. We are a dynamic duo, sister best friends forever. Thank you for being you, I treasure it, and what the future holds.

I would also like to shout out to all my haters. Everyone has them and the better you do in business and in life the more you get. These are all the people that have tried to keep me down. That tried to hold me back from my dreams. You have all given me the strength and determination to be the best that I can be.

To all three of my children, each one of you have such amazing qualities and I love you all more than anything. Zackary you are strong and amazing, you never give up. I love watching you achieve the dreams that you have, and I know you will achieve all of them! Mikayla you have a spirit just like my mom, its caring and deep. You set your mind to something and you make it happen. Johnny my youngest. You have some time still to find what it is that you will set the world on fire with, but so far you have been a blessing to us all. You have such a great sense of humor and a personality that makes everyone love you. I honestly have the best kids! As your mom I couldn't be prouder, my thanks to each of you because of you I strive to be a better person every day.

And I will also like to thank all my close friends. You know who you are, and I'm blessed to have you in my life. I reach for more every day because of the support from my friends. The saying is true "we are stronger together" and that we are!

About Lisa Scola

Stepping outside my comfort zone is something I have been doing my entire life. Going all the way back to child hood, life has always presented challenges to overcome and getting through them is something I share throughout this book. Nothing worthwhile is ever just handed to you, the foot work is what makes getting to where you want to be the most rewarding.

I love to help others, not only in business but in their personal life as well. To be the best that we can be in everything we do is a chapter written for Success, and we can all write our own chapter every day of our lives. I believe after reading what I share you may be on a faster track to accomplishing those goals and living your dreams will be more of a reality.

The words in this book are mine, I was not born to be a writer and don't plan on changing my career any time soon (giggle) but I do love to share my experience, my strength and my hopes with anyone and everyone who may be looking for a bit of inspiration. Let me also thank the editors of UImpact for making it much easier on me in achieving this dream of publishing my own book.

I'm a divorced mom with three beautiful children, I needed to make life adjustments to figure out how to not only live my dreams but raise my children as well. Being successful in business has nothing to do with luck and everything to do with commitment.

When I was growing up I was an Ice Skater and like any sport that you pursue competitively you must commit hours upon hours to it to achieve the success you want to achieve. You invest money in the best skates and hire the best instructors to help you. Direct Sales isn't any different. You need to invest in yourself to learn as much as you can, and you need to put money back into the business to get money out.

The tools that I have used along the way are in this book, not all of them but the most important ones. As you read this book take a moment and write notes in the chapters everywhere I leave room. Highlight what stands out the most and go back and revisit it as much as you need to until you get exactly what you need from it. This is something I do in every self-help and inspirational book that I read myself. It has been an amazing tool that has attributed to my growth. You know the saying "feed your mind what you want it to think" keep positive notes everywhere you work, it also helps to keep your mind from steering off into the negative.

I share regularly in my Facebook group Success with Scola and I encourage you to join it and follow my story. I also have a YouTube channel that I can upload videos to that will encourage and help to push you out of those comfort zones that we all get stuck in. All my Social media links and groups are listed here. I look forward to continuing my journey with you through one of my many social media channels.

Connect with Lisa:

Blog: www.lisascola.com
Support group: www.facebook.com/groups/successwithscola
Continued training: www.youtube.com/successwithscola
Shop online with me: www.youravon.com/avonlisas

Twitter.com/avonlisa
Facebook.com/avonlisas
Linkedin.com/lisa-scola

NOTES

NOTES

NOTES

NOTES

NOTES

NOTES

NOTES

NOTES

Made in the USA
Columbia, SC
12 October 2018